Spirit Orb Phenomena

Fact or Fiction?

To order additional copies, please contact us.
BookSurge, LLC
www.booksurge.com
1-866-308-6235
orders@booksurge.com

Spirit Orb Phenomena
Fact or Fiction?

Anthony Kevan Sercombe

Dedication

I wish to dedicate this book to my wife Denise and my three children, Naomi, Jamie and Kevan. Thanks to their support and understanding throughout, has given me the motivation to complete this book and to achieve most of my life set goals.

Thank you!

Contents

Introduction

The reason for undertaking this investigation adopting a theoretical and practical approach is simply because after having captured these light anomalies with my new digital camera no one seemed to deliver a satisfying explanation. In fact there were so many interpretations that frankly I was perhaps more puzzled than when I originally started. However, this increased my motivation and interest providing an excellent learning opportunity in seeking answers to my questions. Initially I approached this issue of spirit orbs with some scepticism and after examining hundreds of websites I decided to undertake this investigation as a personal challenge.

The aim is to understand their true nature and purpose, attempt to clarify the existing confusion and conflicting theories found in the literature and share this information with others in an endeavour to expand our knowledge on these mysterious balls of light.

One has found countless explanations that suggest what these intriguing orbs may be, and among these are ghosts, spirits, extraterrestrials, guides, angels, other life forms and secret government weapons. Others believe that they are simply defects and processing errors by the digital and traditional 35mm cameras. Others insist they are deliberate hoaxes as quite convincing photographs of such phenomena can be produced by close up photography of particles of dust, rain etc.

Within the literature and photographs on orbs examined there seems to be a correlation between the orbs, ghosts and haunted places (i.e. cemeteries). I have deliberately used the term spirit orb throughout as there is a clear difference. A ghost is the energy of a person that has died and has failed to, or chose to stay on the earth plane as they do not acknowledge that they are dead. They are energies related to haunted places. On the other hand a spirit is an energy that comes from the light from a higher dimension and could be related to friends and family, guides etc. However, in my opinion, although paranormal activity may be related to spirits it should not be consider as "haunting".

One unfortunately does not have a complete explanation and therefore rather than take a shallow dive into what apparently seems a complicated subject, an in depth exploration, discussion and analysis has be undertaken. Most of the data has been retrieved from the World Wide Web as there is an abundance of material relating to spirit orbs. Furthermore, the literature will be supported by a variety of photographs mainly taken within my home, also included are some observations, numerous questions answered and hopefully will be read with an open mind.

All photographs illustrated within have been taken with a 4.0 mega pixel digital camera and have been shown to several individuals such as a photographer and a psychic medium. The former considered some to be paranormal as they posed no explanation, the latter believes they spirit energies and in my opinion whatever they maybe are indeed quite intriguing.

What are Spirit Orbs?

Perhaps, defining and describing what spirit orbs are, is the best way to commence this explorations and analysis of the various conflicting and confusing theories, available within the literature reviewed.

The Longman Dictionary of Contemporary English [Online] defines orb as,

"a bright ball-shaped object"

http://www.ldoceonline.com

Cambridge Dictionaries [Online] claims an orb to be,

"something in the shape of a sphere"

http://www.dictioniary.cambridge.org

and the Merriam-Webster Online Dictionary offers several definitions such as,

"Something circular, a spherical body or a spherical celestial body"

http://www.m-w.com

Perhaps a more explicit explanation may be found in the Encarta encyclopaedia

[Online] describing orb as a soul suggesting the following,

"In many religions and philosophies, the immaterial element that, together with the material body, constitutes the human individual. In general, the soul is conceived as an inner, vital, and spiritual principle, the source of all bodily functions and particularly of mental activities. Belief in some kind of soul that can exist apart from the body is found in all known cultures. In many contemporary non-literate societies, human beings are said to have several souls sometimes as many as seven located in different parts of the body and having diverse functions."

http://www.uk.encarta.msn.com

In my opinion these definitions are rather vague and therefore my attempt to define spirit orbs is as follows;

"Usually a spherical shape of different sizes and colours viewed as circular on film, consisting of plasma and other elements producing electromagnetic energy that may rarely be seen with the naked eye."

Spirit orbs or "BOLs" (Balls of light) are commonly described as hovering or floating, circular, rounded, spherical balls of energy and light. The spirit orbs are made of plasma and consist of a complex plasmoid spherical energy structure of millions of unknown elements and emitting electro magnetic energy (Plate 1). Basically, as electrons within the plasmoid convert to light and electricity and are magnetic, they may be assumed to be an, electrical-magnetic phenomena.

Plate 1:

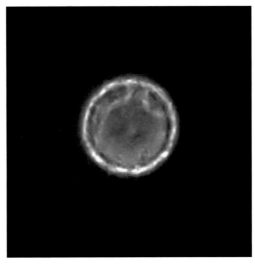

Shows a well defined spirit orb emitting a purplish electro magnetic energy.

These orbs of different sizes often have well defined inner and outer perimeters dividing the inner and outer mantles (Plate 2) and can have different tones of colours at the centre, however, white or grey seem to be dominant (Plate 3).

Plate 2:

Note the outer and inner walls. The perimeter also referred to as shell at times.

Plate 3:

A cluster of orbs varying from transparency to different densities of white.

There are 3 core theories or school of thoughts that classify spirit orbs, these are as follows:

Theory One (The orb is the spirit)

Spirit orbs are believed to be the soul or spirit energy of a person or animal departed from the earth plane. When the physical body dies, the spirit or soul crosses over in another state, keeping all memories, personality, emotions and intelligence. Therefore life continues in a different form. The spirit world seems to be surrounding us, however, at a different vibration than physical matter. Furthermore, although the spirit orb has no physical form it may occupy a physical body.

They may be successful in full materialisation, but it is more common to show themselves as balls of light.

Apparently some people suggest that human spirit orbs appear larger than some of the other types of orbs and usually seen between eye-level and ceiling height (Plate 4). This theory can also be associated with electromagnetic meter (EMF) readings present during spirit activity.

Plate 4:

A large pale white orb taken several meters away from lens.

Theory Two (The orb is the energy the spirit utilises)

The spirit orb is not the spirit at all but the energy the spirit uses for manifestation. This may be the reason when they are captured in clusters (Plates 5, 6 and 7) In this theory the orb is the energy transferred from the sources available (i.e. batteries). This theory too can also be associated with electromagnetic meter (EMF) readings present during spirit activity. Further discussion on how orbs obtain their energy can be found in Chapter Six, Where do Spirit Orbs obtain their Energy?

Plate 5:

Cluster of mainly small orbs, well spaced out.

Plate 6:

This group of very small orbs seem to be more active than in the previous plate.

Plate 7:

A large cluster of mainly transparent medium sized spirit orbs. Note the moving white one towards the bottom right of the picture.

Theory Three (Camera, processing error and pseudo orbs)

This theory is perhaps for the sceptics, where the main belief is that there is nothing paranormal about spirit orbs as they have explanations. Further discussion on this issue may be found in Chapter Seven, Spirit Orb Photography and Chapter Eight, Pseudo Orbs.

Summary

I firmly believe that the three theories are correct depending on the circumstances. There is a need to seriously rule out any pseudo orbs purely because what is then left behind might be spirit orbs and therefore worth investigating further. However, my opinion is that not all orbs are spirits and therefore feel that although some are not, they are possible support in the form of energy for those who are. In other words theory one and two merged together explains my opinion explicitly, obviously after having ruled out the possibility of pseudo orbs.

I also feel that spirit orbs have a conscious and are trying to communicate with us in varied ways. Interesting enough all the majority of the photographs have been taken at home, however prior to the writing of this book very few orbs were captured. Do they have a conscious and have they cooperated to facilitate my work, or is all this a massive coincidence? An interesting and an amazing concept.

Other Types of Orbs
(Non Spirit Orbs)

The literature suggests that other types of orbs have been confused with spirit orbs due to the generalisation of the term. I do not wish to go down this road but it is crucial to comment on them to again clarify the distinction.

Unexplained balls of light have been documented for hundreds of centuries. The various terms used for these phenomena are, earth lights, spook lights, ghost lights, fairy lights, corpse candles, fox fire and perhaps the most similar in composition to spirit orbs are balls of lighting. However, unlike the theories of spirit orbs, these light anomalies are produced by earth itself (storms, volcanoes, earthquakes). They have a range of colours and tones, are much larger than spirit orbs and are seen with the naked eye in an outdoor scenario usually in the sky and even above the clouds. They may adopt different shapes, appear as luminous vapours, display glowing tails, move randomly and sometimes even explode.

Apparently the Egyptians named them 'sun boats' and thought they were souls. Another belief related to these orbs is that they are UFOs from a higher dimensional level of existence.

What is clear is that their characteristics and composition are different to that of spirit orbs and therefore let us not jump onto a band wagon in relation to this term.

The Appearances of Spirit Orbs
Shape

Spirit orbs are usually seen on film as circular flat balls of light (Plates 8, 9 and 10) due to the 2D images produced by 35mm or digital cameras, but in fact orbs are spherical. However, although a circular round shape is perhaps the most common form the spirit orbs adopts it is not uncommon to capture them in a variety of shapes such as oval (Plate 11), tiny bright flashing pin point type (Plate 12) and some paranormal enthusiast claim even triangular. Personally I have not experienced or captured on camera any spirit orb in a triangular form and therefore I would suggest that although the spirit orb can be a paranormal phenomenon, some orbs caught on cameras may pose a simple explanation falling into the pseudo orb category.

Scientists can not fully explain why the spirit orb is spherical, as electrons will not form a sphere on their own. They need something to hold them together, or will immediately disseminate out in all directions. Perhaps, this form of energy responds in the same manner as water in zero gravity conditions being pulled together to form a sphere. However, what is known is that the energy configuration of the spirit orb resembles that of the ball of lightning (Plate 13).

Furthermore, it is not understood why the spirit orbs develop prominent outer and inner ring structures (Plates 14 and 15), when energy spaces seem to be occupied and the orbs become a denser looking light colour usually whiter (Plate 16 and 17).

Plate 8:

A common photograph of a single orb, very flat and circular.

Plate 9:

A medium sized orb, hovering at eye level, resembling a white disc.

Plate 10:

A large circular ball of light.

Plate 11:

This is an example of an oval or diamond shaped orb.

Plate 12:

This image shows a pin point orb at the top of the picture. Usually they are brighter and even smaller. Enlarging pictures to observe the images in greater detail is essential if not these minute orbs will be missed.

Plate 13:

Perhaps a smaller version of the 'ball of lightening'. This orb is charged with electrons and reflecting impressive amount of light.

Plate 14:

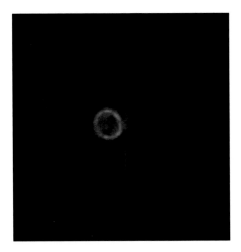

A small spirit orb that has its outer and inner walls illuminated. The space between these two walls outer mantle too is illuminated.

Plate 15:

Example of a very small orb with perimeter and inner wall illuminated.

Plate 16:

A pale white orb perhaps, becoming denser as it builds up its energy level.

Plate 17:

A dense orb, although it is still translucent.

Colour

Most of the spirit orbs captured on camera seem to be white (Plates 18 and 19) giving off light apparently brighter when fully materialised (Plates 20, 21 and 22) or greyish transparent (Plates 23, 24, 25 and 26). However, several seemed to be of various colours, often orbs are red (Plates 27 28 and 29), pink (Plates 30 and 31), green (Plate 32), blue (Plates 33 and 34) and many other colours. Another fascinating feature is the glowing aura usually a purple colour radiating from the perimeter (Plates 35, 36 37 and 38). Furthermore, spirit orbs have many electrons moving in their mantle thus will discharge a significant amount of electromagnetic energy (Plates 39 and 40) that can be detected by EMF equipment, digital cameras and psychic individuals.

Plate 18:

A white spirit orb just in front of the lamp, several transparent ones also visible within this image.

Plate 19:

A small dense white orb floating at ceiling level.

Plate 20:

A fascinating spirit orb, manifesting to what I believe is its full density potential.

Plate 21:

An orb to almost full density status yet not reflecting much light.

Plate 22:

This orb is in the process of becoming denser. Note that the lamp may be seen behind the orb.

Plate 23:

A good example of a large greyish transparent spirit orb.

Plate 24:

Several sized orbs hovering between eye and ceiling level, all are transparent.

Plate 25:

Four large spirit orbs, however, three transparent ones.

Plate 26:

Several transparent orbs at different levels.

Plate 27:

A red orb in slight motion as small trail is visible.

Plate 28:

Red orb on the right side of picture with denser inner and outer walls.

Plate 29:

Small red orb close to the floor.

Plate 30:

A pink orb with diffused borders.

Plate 31:

A small pink orb seen at ceiling level.

Plate 32:

A green orb moving close to the floor.

Plate 33:

Blue orb in fast circular motion.

Plate 34:

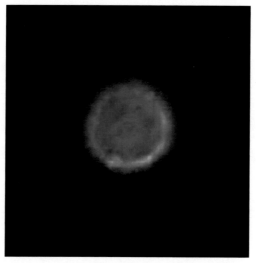

A small blue orb.

Plate 35:

A dense white orb with well defined inner and outer walls, where a small purple glowing aura can be seen around the shell.

Plate 36:

The aura is present here even though the orb is still translucent.

Plate 37:

An opaque dense white orb with beautiful glowing aura radiating from its perimeter.

Plate 38:

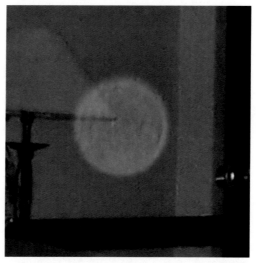

A medium sized orb with a weak aura.

Plate 39:

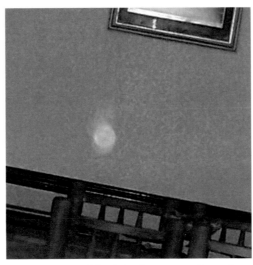

This small white orb has left a trail behind suggesting the trajectory it has taken.

Plate 40:

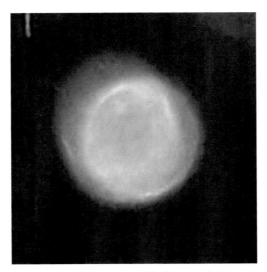

Note the amount of energy discharged for propulsion.

Size

When recorded on film, the orb size is often confused because the photo is only 2D and its size is dependent on the distance from the lens the orb is when captured by the camera. Size will depend much on the level of energy acquired however some claim that the human spirit may appear larger than some of the other types of orbs (Plates 41, 42, 43, 44 and 45). The different sizes observed can be from a pinpoint (Plate 46) to an average of fifteen to eighteen centimetres in diameter, however, rarely up to 30 centimetres (Plate 47) have been documented, yet I found that the medium (Plates 48, 49, 50 and 51) and small (Plates 52 and 53) sized ones were more commonly captured on camera.

Plate 41:

A large single transparent spirit orb.

Plate 42:

A large spirit orb and smaller one just below. An interesting observation is that they do not seem to reflect themselves onto mirrors.

Plate 43:

Two large orbs at different distances just above eye level.

Plate 44:

Four large orbs one of them is white and the others are transparent.

Plate 45:

Large single orb in front of lamp.

Plate 46:

Several pin point orbs seen in this picture.

Plate 47:

The clarity of this photograph is not good but it's the biggest orb I have ever captured on camera. Note the size compared to the basketball board.

Plate 48:

A white medium sized orb.

Plate 49:

This spirit orb is medium sized and translucent.

Plate 50:

This medium sized orb seems a white round disc.

Plate 51:

A medium sized orb.

Plate 52:

Several small orbs at different distances and densities.

Plate 53:

Two small orbs. The one at the lower end of the image is moving randomly.

Texture

Spirit orbs seem to appear with a variety of inner textures, fascinating to admire. A common type resembles that of an animal cell (Plates 54 and 55). However , among these textures there are types that look like cotton wool (Plates 56, 57 and 58) others rough like mountain ranges (Plates 59 and 60) others smooth (Plate 61) and many more different and fascinating patterns.

Plate 54:

A transparent spirit orb. However, the black hole (Jet) within the inner mantle reminds me of an animal cell.

Plate 55:

Another example of an animal cell appearance. Note that this orb has two Jets in its mantle.

Plate 56:

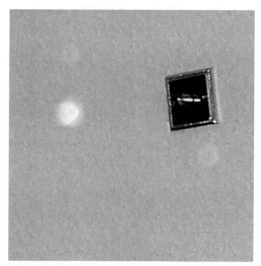

This small orb takes a cotton wool swab appearance.

Plate 57:

When orb adopts this appearance there are no defined inner or outer walls.

Plate 58:

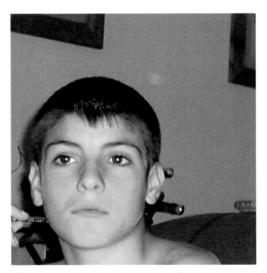

A very small cotton wool type of orb over my son's head.

Plate 59:

This texture I found to be uncommon.

Plate 60:

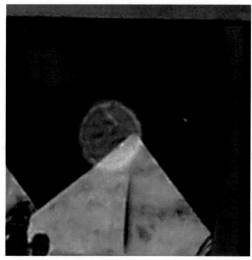

A mountain range appearance is all I can say here.

Plate 61:

A dense, smooth and white spirit orb.

Extra

Orbs are sometimes captured on camera with a fine mist or smoke around them (Plates 62 and 63), apparently this is when a physical apparition is attempted. A popular theory is that when the spirit is moving about it uses the lowest form of energy possible, therefore assuming the shape of an orb, but when it is no longer in motion, the spirit energy that is compressed within the orb is released and this spirit energy expands into what is named as Ecto-Vapour or Ectoplasmic Vapour. Another interesting observation is that some orbs will contain more than one soul and when its spirit energy is released, several orbs emerge from one single orb.

Plate 62:

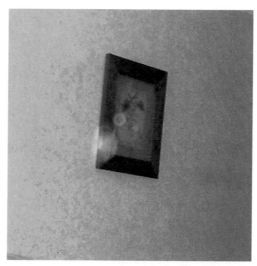

The small orb is within the picture frame and the mist is almost directly below.

Plate 63:

A beautifully brightly illuminated spirit orb accompanied by a bluish mist. According to psychics within this mist a full apparition may occur.

These series of photographs illustrated (Plates 64, 65, 66 and 67) allows me to suggest that beams of light from perhaps a different dimension or plane are projected to the physical (earth) plane to allow the passage and entry of spirit orbs. This reminds me of several scenes from the movie "Ghost" produced by Paramount Pictures (1990) where beams of light are seen with emerging hovering bright balls of light.

Plate 64:

This is one of four pictures (plates 65, 66, and 67) of approximately 20 photographs taken in a series. As you can see there are no paranormal anomalies in this one.

Plate 65:

In this picture two beams of light are seen in each side of the room. In fact the right is more obvious than the left one as it radiates from the ceiling just above the T.V. to the sofa at an angle.

Plate 66:

In the picture immediately after, the beams of light disappear but in its place two orbs are seen in its place instead. I have caught these phenomena several times in different locations.

Plate 67:

The scene is back to normal again.
The most remarkable ones are perhaps the most rarely photographed which are those that often have a more detailed and complex appearance within the inner mantle, which can at times resembles faces and or figures even to the naked eye (Plates 68, 69, 70, 71, 72, 73 and 74).

Plate 68:

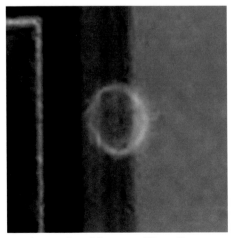

An orb with a smiling face.

Plate 69:

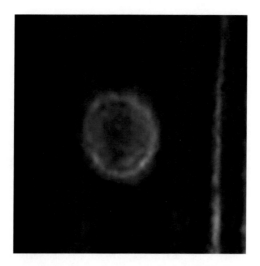

Look well within this blue orb as it seems to resemble a bald man with marked ears.

Plate 70:

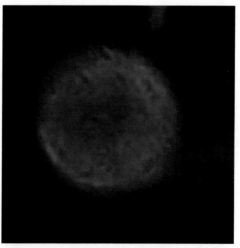

There is a definite face that is forming almost at the centre. However, if you look carefully around, you may agree that there could be more than one face within this orb.

Plate 71:

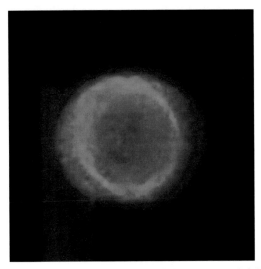

This red orb has male facial features within it.

Plate 72:

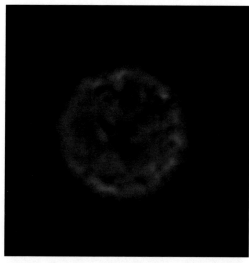

Part of a face can be seen at the centre of this orb.

Plate 73:

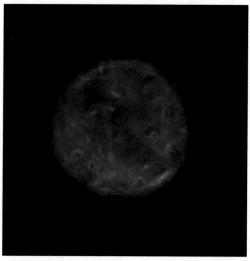

A large face can be seen within this orb.

Plate 74:

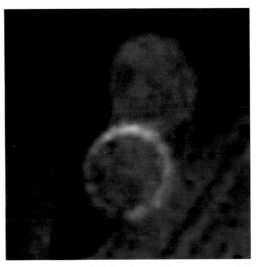

This picture was taken at work in pitch black environment. Note the two orbs have quite detailed faces in them.

According to mediums, spirit orbs can be sensed and/or heard. The sound they make is a super-high tone, mainly heard within the head or inside or past the one ear and out through another, perhaps a frequency beyond normal hearing?

Why can Spirit Orbs Move?

These hovering spirit orbs, as far as mass is concerned have a small amount of weight and inertia and has the ability to move electrons in their outer mantle to a concentrated location, which in turn forces some electrons to be expelled through the black holes in the mantle also known as Jets (Plates 75 and 76). This action is therefore sufficient to propel them very rapidly in any direction (Plates 77, 78, 79 and 80). The ejected electrons will release photons in the process and may be viewed as a trail. I have recorded this rapid event with my digital camera. This process is not usually seen by the naked eye.

Plate 75:

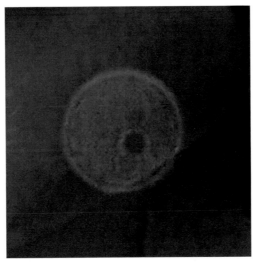

There is a clear jet in this picture. It is not uncommon to capture them with two jets within their mantle.

Plate 76:

An enlarged image that shows the jet clearly.

Plate 77:

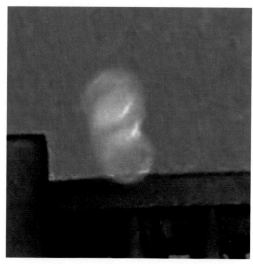

White orb in a zigzag motion.

Plate 78:

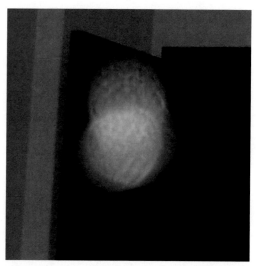

Very large orb leaving a trail as it moves downwards.

Plate 79:

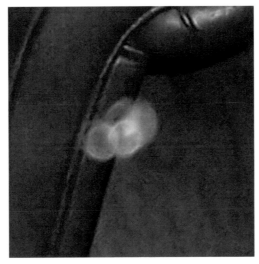

Orb going round in circles.

Plate 80:

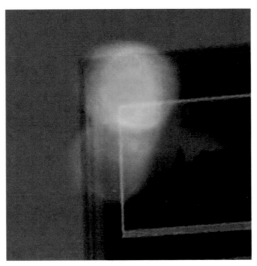

Fascinating orb in upward motion.

The flash present in modern digital cameras, have an intense burst but short duration capability, in fact, between one thousandth and ten thousandth of a second enough to capture the fastest moving spirit orb (Plate 81), however, not all orbs move rapidly. Orbs seem to move in a random manner (Plate 82, 83 and 84), others especially the tiny ones travel in a linear way (Plates 85 and 86), yet others seem to propel themselves in a circular fashion (Plate 87). When several types of orbs of different sizes and displaying a variety of movements are captured on camera at the same time an intriguing and fascinating result can be admired, in fact it reminds me of a firework display (Plates 88 and 89).

Plate 81:

Several fast moving orbs.

Plate 82:

Orb moving randomly.

Plate 83:

This orb seems to be following my daughter around.

Plate 84:

Randomly moving orb.

Plate 85:

Behind the author a straight line of light may be observed.

Plate 86:

Very small orb travelling fast in a linear fashion.

Plate 87:

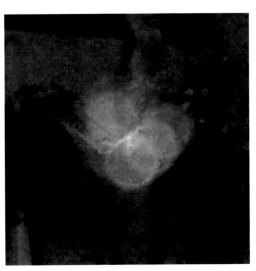

This moderate sized orb was going round in circles.

Plate 88:

A cluster of orbs.

Plate 89:

Several types of orbs collectively.

A personal observation is when moving orbs are captured on still camera they appear to leave a trail behind and the small pin points of light tend to move the fastest. This type of orb may be observed as a small white pin point sphere shooting through a room and/or solid object, such as through a wall or a lamp (Plates 90 and 91),

Plate 90:

An enlarged picture to show that orb is going through lamp.

Plate 91:

Small orb moving within reeds.

Where do Spirit Orbs obtain their Energy?

There are many common sources of energy (Electrons) that the orbs "feed on" as they need this for moving and manifesting. These sources may include electric power lines, heat energy, atmospheric storms, batteries, people and from orb to orb upon contact.

The concept is that small spirit orbs take up the least amount of energy and apparitions and other larger and denser orbs take up the most.

Within the literature there seems to be a relation between the winter cold stormy seasons with spirits finding it easier to take on shapes other than orbs perhaps due to the abundance of electrons available from the atmospheric storms. Some believe that the spirit may not even be aware they need the energy therefore making it a natural sub conscious process of acquiring their energy requirements.

Spirit Orb Photography

The best and perhaps most popular manner for capturing images of spirit orbs is using digital cameras (Charged Coupled Devices), but some have been known to have been captured with the use of the traditional 35mm cameras and film. The benefits of the digital camera to the "paranormal enthusiast" cannot go unmentioned. The ability to take countless pictures and to immediately examine them proves to be advantageous and cost effective in contrast to the alternative of sending films to be processed. However, a more interesting point to make is that digital cameras are more successful in capturing spirit orbs than the traditional cameras and this is not because more pictures are taken at no cost, but the prime reason is that the CCDs (The camera's seeing ability) detects frequency of light beyond the human eye. Furthermore, the human eye can approximately see in the range of 400 nanometres along the violet end of the light spectrum to 700 nanometres along the red end of the spectrum. Digital cameras can see in the range of 500 nanometres in the violet end and can go as far as the infra red spectrum at approximately 1100 nanometres, therefore the ranges clearly show that CCDs go well beyond the human visual acuity. The digital cameras can not obviously have film-processing errors. However, some people claim that the orbs on a digital camera are an error or defect in the digital processing of the image. According to the manufacturer when that error or defect occurs in digital photographs, the objects tend to be squared in nature, not round and they cannot be semi-transparent, as the picture is composed of pixels.

Many people claim that orb activity is best captured in total darkness, perhaps darkness provides a blank background which makes it easier to pick an orb out. However, through my own experience spirit orbs can best be captured with dim light, but are present both indoors and outdoors during daylight (Plate 92) and at night (Plate 93), irrespective of time and using flash at all times. There is a scientific reason for this as will be explained.

Plate 92:

This daylight photo was taken in Tunisia. Note the orb at the bottom left hand side of the picture.

Plate 93:

Several orbs caught outdoors and at night in this hospital patio.

The process that makes spirit orbs photographable is known as fluorescence or photoluminescence, a term usually related with minerals. The orbs can be captured on camera when exposed to a large number of Photons (green) from a light source such as a camera flash and are then absorbed by electrons within the orb itself which then move to a higher energy orbit. When the electrons return to their original orbit, new photons (red) are released at a slightly lower frequency. This release happens within microseconds. Basically as the light from the flash penetrates through each layer of the orb, there are further own photons generated that will in turn be spontaneously emitted back to the digital camera. On occasions when the orb absorbs a greater density of electrons around the outer mantle it may be photographed too showing this as bright luminous band (s) along the perimeter (Plates 94 and 95).

Plate 94:

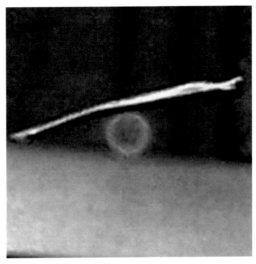

A small orb with bright shell.

Plate 95:

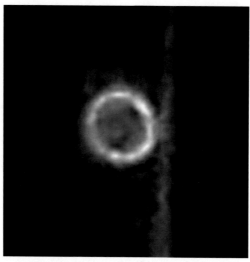

A small orb with luminous inner and outer walls.

Pseudo Orbs

During my investigation I discovered that not all orb photographs are necessarily paranormal in nature. These explained images of false orbs (not paranormal) have been labelled as Pseudo Orbs. There are a number of photographic anomalies and artefacts that may resemble spirit orbs, such as dust particles, pollen, moisture in the air, ice crystals, snow flakes, rain drops, fog, mist, hairs, feathers, air-borne seeds, cobwebs, flying insects and other weather related anomalies.

If any of these examples are captured close to the lens and with flash and/or sunlight, they will be grossly illuminated and/or out of focus and when viewed they will resemble spirit orbs. My own experiment confirmed this. A moth several meters away from the lens produced a convincing example (Plate 96).

Plate 96:

The moth reflects the light from the flash resembling an orb. However, notice the shadow on the wall. Orbs do not cast shadows.

Lens Flare may also produce pseudo orbs. This will occur both with digital and traditional cameras. Lens Flare is the result of taking photographs into a light source (i.e. Sun) (Plate 97) or towards a reflective surface (i.e. Glass, metal) (Plate 98).Other possible causes to consider could be car headlights, fireworks and torches.

Plate 97:

This photo shows coloured orbs produced from direct sunlight.

Plate 98:

Although there is a spirit orb at the bottom left of this image the pseudo orb is the bright reflection at the end of corridor caused by glass door.

Tobacco smoke too, when photographs rendered, may well appear as ecto- plasmic vapour.

Dirt and moisture in or on the lens or a strap or finger in front of the lens may produce photos resembling paranormal activity. In 35mm traditional photographs ball of light may be caused by crystallization of the developing fluid and chemical stains on the film itself as they leave a convincing circular defect on the print.

Due to the advancement of computer technology many pictures could also be faked.

Photographic Method and Environment

To reduce or perhaps eliminate all the variables (Pseudo orbs) encountered with outdoor photography, I have deliberately used my home specifically the sitting room which approximately measures 8 x 4 meters. Secondly, orbs are mainly related to haunted places with a keen interest by many to obtain pictures from cemeteries. My home (Not haunted) is only 10 years old and I have been the sole owner, this in itself will disassociate spirit orbs from haunted places (Ghost orbs). There are other advantages to consider using this stable environment. One is that the furniture, sofa, lamp, walls, tables, doors etc provide a reasonable landmark to judge distance of the orb(s) from the lens and most importantly facilitates the estimation of size(s) perhaps more accurately. The second point is that there is full control over the lighting used in this room and therefore photographs may be taken from pitch black to a bright sunlight environment. Although many recommend pitch black settings, I personally found that using dim lighting was a more successful method.

It is necessary that a base line be established prior to any investigations of this sort and therefore numerous photographs were taken and examined for and discovered the areas where reflections and other anomalies occur. Common sense is also required so, no smoking and the elimination of draughts was also necessary.

As an amateur I experimented and learnt using my own camera and seeing how this device displays anomalies such as dust. However, they were several shapes but none really resembled a spirit orb. Also you may reveal through this process if the camera produces the same configuration of an orb which in this case it did not. I also found that by using the flash it was more successful to capture this phenomena however, some were captured without flash. Also by taking photos in sequence helped to compare and contrast each picture. If there is dust it should be present in every image. An interesting observation I encountered was that orbs rarely appear in consecutive photographs. Further investigation was undertaken on the computer using a basic viewer. This is essential and useful because the image may be enlarged and further findings noted and pseudo orbs identified or excluded. A total of 10,000 photographs were taken in a period of three months. These were then examined and approximately 500 were classified and saved although 98 have been displayed within this book. While these amazing paranormal images presents, some of the best spirit orb photographs taken they are not hard evidence that spirits are orbs.

Problems with Spirit Orbs

Spirit orbs have and radiate electro magnetic energy and although they are not hot in themselves may have a heating effect through the objects they pass depending much on the level of energy (Electrons) at that given instance in time.

The spirit orbs can without any problem pass through solid objects. In doing so they may heat up the object considerably but, not to the point of burning them due to the limited amount of electrons they can carry. They may also affect or damage electrical devices, in other words lights may flicker, televisions may switch off etc.

Spirit orbs are normally harmless and have relatively no wish to inflict harm on anyone or anything nor do they have much of an awareness to act as such. However, spirits have been known to move objects around, but truthfully they are quite limited to what they can do in the form they exist.

On the other hand, some may view these orbs as annoying as they keep showing up almost anywhere thus spoiling the photograph(s). In certain circumstances cameras under warranty have be replaced by new ones from the manufactures but the same anomalies have been reported.

Communication

There is much debate about whether orbs are the spirit itself or just signs that a spirit is present and trying to communicate with the physical world. Irrespective of this issue mediums claim that the spirit world wants to contact us more than we want to contact them, so they will manifest at any opportunity, these beings love us and want us to see them. Therefore, the sprit energy will take advantage of any method of communication if it is appropriate, and embrace our technology as a means of doing so.

Mediums claim to talk (Telepathically) to them regularly. When mediums actually communicate with spirits or spirit orbs depending on your belief, the spirit often manifest itself as it was when living as a human or animal. This means that a medium can describe them as they remember themselves. This would include colour of eyes, hair and skin, height personality and character, how they crossed over, memories of their life experiences etc. However, this is what the spirit or spirit orb recalls about their life, and recreates it so the medium can convey the information to help recognition for the sitter.

Some claim that when this form of communication is established the spirit orb is extremely close to the medium's aura. And apparently some of the photographs within some websites show the orb linking with the medium through a hair like projection from its shell (Perimeter). Unfortunately, I have not had the opportunity to photograph spirit orbs during this event.

Conclusion

With so many unanswered questions still waiting to be addressed I personally feel that science through the Unified Field Plasmoids Theory may offer more research answers that need to be discovered. However, perhaps a multidisciplinary approach involving researchers, scientists, mediums, paranormal investigators, and professional photographers etc, could formulate the right combination of expertise for a research project in the fields of lower tropospheric plasma physics and quantum mechanics. With all these diverse experts to this wide open and exciting field of research, the outcome could unravel astonishing results.

However, concurrently whatever you believe spirit orbs are, is perhaps entirely up to you, at least they seem fascinating, friendly, harmless and intriguing to admire.

Glossary

(Adapted from Merriam-Webster Online Dictionary http://www.m-w.com)

Aura: A luminous radiation, an energy field that is held to emanate from a living being.

Ecto plasmic vapour: A substance held to produce spirit materialization and telekinesis.

Electrons : An elementary particle consisting of a charge of negative electricity equal to about 1.602×10^{-19} coulomb and having a mass when at rest of about 9.109534×10^{-28} gram or about $1/1836$ that of a proton.

Fluorescence: Luminescence that is caused by the absorption of radiation at one wavelength followed by nearly immediate re radiation usually at a different wavelength and that ceases almost at once when the incident radiation stops or the radiation emitted.

Haunted: to have a disquieting or harmful effect on, or to visit or inhabit as a ghost.

Manifest: an occult phenomenon, or an apparition of a paranormal energy.

Mantle: The mantle of molluscs and brachiopods secretes the shell if one is present. It also forms a mantle cavity between itself and the body. The inner space of an orb contain within the perimeter wall (Shell).

Paranormal: Not scientifically explainable.

Phenomenon: An observable fact or event, or an object or aspect known through the senses rather than by thought or intuition, or a temporal or a fact or event of scientific interest susceptible of scientific description and explanation.

Photoluminescence: The low-temperature emission of light (as by a chemical or physiological process), or light produced by luminescence.

Photons: A unit of intensity of light at the retina equal to the illumination received per square millimetre of a pupillary area from a surface having a brightness of one candle per square meter, or a quantum of electromagnetic radiation.

Pixel: The smallest element of a light-sensitive device, such as cameras that use charge-coupled devices.

Plasmoid: A collection of charged particles (as in the atmospheres of stars or in a metal) containing about equal numbers of positive ions and electrons and exhibiting some properties of a gas but differing from a gas in being a good conductor of electricity and in being affected by a magnetic field.

Pseudo: Being apparently rather than actually as stated.

Sitter: One that sits awaiting or receiving a reading from a medium.

Telepathically: Communication from one mind to another by extrasensory means.

Tropospheric: The lowest densest part of the earth's atmosphere in which most weather changes occur and temperature generally decreases rapidly with altitude and which extends from the surface to the bottom of the stratosphere.